C000007958

Fort (40) Far

Conversation About How Cumbria's

Landscape Is Changing

Theresa V Massey

For nearly a century and a half, the family farm's total demise has been confidently predicted, and it still is today. Even though many have died out by the 21st century, it is remarkable that so many have survived in so many different countries. Many observers believe that the continued existence of these non-corporate units of production in what is now referred to as "late capitalism" is anomalous, if not archaic. The book concludes with an integrated explanation, but in this first chapter, we explain why it was anticipated that they would disappear during a much earlier stage of capitalist evolution. The term "family farm" is then clarified. A few more significant issues are discussed in detail in subsequent chapters.

Farming and capitalism: the model for the classic "agrarian question" In Britain between the 15th and 18th centuries, the typical farmer became a tenant who paid rent on leasehold land and worked it himself or with hired laborers. This changed the farmer from a peasant who worked strips of land in exchange for services or quit-rent to a lordly holder. In the meantime, a growing group of people, including descendants of feudal lords and owners of a variety of businesses, had acquired land. Instead of being obligated to provide services to the lords, labor became wage-dependent and "free" to pursue other endeavors. This process took a long time, but in comparison to other nations, it moved faster and further in Britain. The "surplus value" of labor—that portion of the product of labor that was not required to be paid to workers for their needs of survival—was accumulated by capitalists after the old feudal bonds were broken and a population of "free" workers was created. They were free to compete with one another in the market and invest the surplus in brand-new sectors. Smith, Adam (1776:

155) had already mentioned that the country's surplus produce in addition to the cultivation equipment's upkeep constitutes the town's means of subsistence. Marx (1867) reinterpreted this necessary relationship and used it as the foundation for explaining and (imperfectly) predicting the global capitalist economy's future.

From Marx to Lenin and Kautsky to farms Marx, an economist, sociologist, and historian, believed that "primitive accumulation" of capital was the initial foundation of capitalism. This was accomplished through enclosures, which involved separating the worker from control of the means of production, whether as owner or renter, in the context of a growing market economy, as he not entirely accurately interpreted the English model in the famous Chapter 24 of Capital I (Marx, 1867). As a result, paid labor was required to produce the commodities that were traded on the market. Therefore, capitalists obtained the means of production on the land, and labor became proletarian.1 The competitive discipline of "market dependence" resulted in improvements and innovations that increased labor and land productivity. The costs of providing food and other raw materials to the expanding urban and other non-agricultural population brought about by capitalist transformation were reduced as a result of this same increase in productivity. The nineteenth-century "agrarian question" centered on the transfer of agricultural surpluses to investment in other economic sectors, particularly industry (Kautsky, 1899; Lenin 1899). Merchants and usurers used a variety of means to acquire farmers' capital. One more was 'inconsistent trade', being the distinction (in labor esteem) between returns for rural and modern

merchandise. In the twentieth century, a similar fundamental question came to dominate a lot of non-Marxist economic thinking about developing nations. Extending taxes on primary produce exports to generate the foreign currency needed to finance industrial development was the most common approach.

While collection gave the assets expected to industry, and the work

'liberated' from the land additionally gave the work to industry, there were significant results among the agrarian populace. These effects occurred regardless of whether formerly feudal lords transformed into capitalist large farmers or whether such farmers emerged as a result of differences among rural landowners. Lenin (1899), elaborating heavily on Marx and following the internal differentiation approach, argued that competitive success would elevate the wealthier peasants to the status of capitalist farmers while the less successful would fall to the level of proletarian labor.2 All aspects of the capitalist economy are competitive. Over time, the "middle peasant" would vanish as a result of the process. He used a large amount of original data on Russian farming to illustrate these arguments. The majority of the data came from inquiries conducted for local and provincial councils (zemstvo), which were established in 1864 following the emancipation of serfs in 1861. Ten of these inquiries provided Lenin with the majority of his information. His analysis of the zemstvo data revealed that Russian peasant farmers had developed significant differences in the use of farm machinery, livestock, and land held and worked. The Russian village economy's apparent "capitalist contradictions" were evident to him.

When Kautsky (1899) expanded his scope to include Europe, he discovered that the liberal economic revolution of the nineteenth century had not generally resulted in the breakdown that Marx had anticipated. Marx viewed the emergence of capitalist/proletarian division in the countryside in the context of already-established trade, treating the emergence of capitalism as primarily in manufacturing. Market rivalry would lean toward the bigger scope maker who was better positioned to embrace the numerous specialized advancements utilizing

wage work. This competition would eliminate the smaller peasant. However, this would take time because farms shrink and grow independently for a variety of reasons. Kautsky and a lot of other people who have used the same argument have said that the big farmer has a big advantage because of economies of scale in production, just like Marx and other writers before him had seen them in industry. Compared to a small farmer, a capitalist farmer could afford to mechanize, utilize labor more effectively, acquire and utilize credit, and utilize scientific advancements more effectively. The large farmer could produce more effectively due to these advantages. In the modern era of neo-liberal free-market economics, the strong preference for capitalist farming is also based on these competitive advantages, which are still widely perceived. However, there have been lengthy and in-depth discussions regarding the issue of how efficient large and small farms are in comparison. Small farms typically have higher yields per hectare than larger farms. While a lot of the modern argument is based on Berry and

Cline's (1979) comparative study, which is now out of date, Griffin et al. () have argued again that smaller farmers have a higher yield advantage, primarily based on modern data from Brazil. 2004). In response, Byres (2004) argues that yield per hectare and yield per unit of labor must be distinguished, and based on the latter, the capitalist farm appears to have a distinct advantage. Bernstein (2006) is careful to point out that scale alone no longer appears to be a major consideration in – at least scholarly – debate when writing about a modern form of the agrarian question.

Friedmann, Chayanov, and the commercial family farm's future Harriet Friedmann (1978a, 1978b, and 1980) doctoral research on the social history of modern wheat farming brought to light an aspect of events that had been surprisingly overlooked in the late nineteenth century in a series of papers. The non-capitalist "middle peasant" in Europe had shown significant resilience in the last quarter of the nineteenth century, but Kautsky (1899) thought this was only temporary. Not at all. Capitalist farms in both Europe and the United States gave way to family-operated farms, not the other way around, when American wheat began to significantly enter the European market in the 1870s and global prices fell. The vast majority of commercial wheat production worldwide was organized through household rather than wage labor by 1935, following the second major period of low prices. However, by the 1870s, capitalism had reached all of the wheat-producing regions that were part of the trade, and most of them already had capitalist farms that relied on wage labor to produce their goods. As a result, wage labor farms and household farms were in direct competition, and during the entire time, the latter prevailed.

Friedmann's lengthy explanation is technical in part.3 In the United States' great plains, harvesting and later threshing machinery were quickly introduced, reducing the need for farm labor. Mechanized farming became feasible for a family labor force of 1.5 men, as family farms increased in size through purchase and rental of machinery suitable for the new average area (about 140 ha after 1920); Inadequate data on female employees have existed and continue to exist. Workers were lured away from the large capitalist farms of the 1870s and 1880s to establish family farms while new land and credit remained available.

Household farms, which did not face either of these constraints, were able to compete with the large farms because they were required to both pay rising wages and generate profits.

At received wheat prices, which converged rapidly between nations and all moved together after the middle of the 1890s, capitalist farmers in Europe had to compete with producers from the United States, Canada, and later Australia and Argentina using household labor. Coercive labor management and the importation of Polish laborers helped German capitalist farmers, who had previously been primarily feudal landlords; They were helped by tariff protection, just like French farmers. British farmers who didn't get this kind of help mostly switched from growing crops to specializing in livestock, which cut down on the need for workers.

In contrast to the German situation, the majority of farmers in the British case were already tenants, and the non-farming owners of the land were responsible for the decline in land values.

The technical conditions were important, but they needed to be weighed against the different social conditions of production in capitalist farms and farms with household labor. Aleksandr Chayanov (1923–1966) used the same zemstvo data as Lenin in his research, but Friedmann also relied on his own inquiries as well as those of his colleagues and students. Chayanov came to the conclusion that the balance between consumers and workers within the household was the primary determinant of the scale of production. He found that the demographic stage of a household, as it first grew and then declined after the young became independent, was the dominant factor in bringing about differentiation between family farms, regardless of their degree of commercial orientation4. We adapted his frequently cited and frequently misunderstood table that summarizes results in the Volokolamsk district, west of Moscow.

Chayanov's explanation relied on the fact that household workers do not receive direct wages but rather consume the product of their labor in the form of money, food, clothing, or both. 4 Asking agrarian questions Table 1.1 Productivity and work intensity in relation to household composition at Volokolamsk, 1910 Consumption per worker Consumption/Worker ratio 1–1.2 1.21–1.4 1.41–1.6 over 1.6 Worker's output (roubles) 131.9 151.5 218.8 283.4 Working days per worker 96.8 102.3 157.2 161.3 Note: Using data from 25 family farms, Chayanov (1966: 78, table 2–8).

mostly industrialist economy for hypothetical purposes. He characterized it as "a family that does not hire outside labor, has a particular area of land available to it, and has its own means of production [i.e. tools, etc.]," and sometimes has to use some of its workers in non-agricultural trades and crafts (Chayanov, 1966: 51). The farm is not structurally required to make a profit. The family unit is viewed as a single, undifferentiated unit of production and consumption. In Marxist terms, it will "reproduce" the farm in order to pay its rent (if any) and taxes, keep the farm running, and satisfy its own demands, but it will not willingly do more than that. The primary driver of the shift in the family farm's consumer-to-worker ratio will be the aging and replacement of families as a result of the demographic process. When comparing costs, returns, and responses among farms operating under different production systems, Kautsky and Chayanov were in fact both using a neo-Darwinist evolutionary approach, formalized by Lawson (2003) as a population–variety–reproduction–selection model, in which market competition leads to selection of the "fittest varieties." In effect, Chayanov was relying on the marginal analysis of neo-classical economics, which states that an equilibrium level

Kautsky was involved in the commodity market and believed that the wage-earning capitalist farm was the best option;

Friedmann largely concurred with Chayanov's assessment of the peasant farm's superiority in terms of its ability to compete in markets for production factors. Ellis (1988a), focusing solely on Chayanov, drew attention to revisions brought about by the "new home economics," which emerged in the 1960s and 1970s. These revisions began by recognizing that households produce their own utilities, whose use values are ultimately derived from their final consumption. When there is a labor market, inputs are not so much determined by preferences as they are by the current wage rate and price level.

This results in opportunity costs of time spent on various activities. In spite of Chayanov's model, this permits choices concerning

work use to be isolated from choices as for money. For instance, an increase in the going market wage will result in a decrease in the use of hired labor, an increase in family farm work, and an increase in the proportion of output consumed at home. The internal logic of the household model is altered by the existence of a labor market, not the least of which is how the household interacts with the economy as a whole. Ellis

(1988a: "The unique mode of economic calculation proposed by Chayanov disappears," according to 139).

However, the Chayanov family always operated within a labor market.

Optimizing competing utilities in a market and natural environment that varied was the goal. Lehmann (1986) describes "capitalist family farms," which rely on family labor and supplementary labor recruited primarily through kinship ties but also invest in machinery specifically to avoid the need to hire labor, in an entertaining discussion of Marxist work on transitions to capitalism among South American peasants that is illuminated by his field work in Ecuador. In this context, he is describing modern family farms all over the world. 2001: Sivakumar 42) would rather think of Indian family farmers as constantly "adapting themselves to changing objectives and Asking agrarian questions 5 constraints," which translates to "satisficing" in modern parlance. Within the limits of production-possibility, they are managing well.

Sivakumar believes that Chayanov's arguments are more convincing than Marxian reasoning or the contemporary complex of ideas that result from applying classical and neo-classical economics to agrarian issues. The "efficient but poor" peasants of Schultz (1964), who were altered under risk to be following a "survival algorithm" (Lipton 1968), are not discussed by Sivakumar. Nevertheless, he incorporates these ideas into a discussion of agriculture's profound uncertainties. Coming from

a foundation of life and exploration in southern India, Sivakumar (2001) reworked

the dynamic issue with regards to 'exchange systems' wherein predominance and reliance, order and area as to the geological

appropriation of assets and their changeability were the basic setting of all

choices. Transaction market construction became special cases due to the competitive market economy's anonymity and Marxist emphasis on rich-poor conflicts of interest. Therefore, he came to the conclusion that a theory of noncapitalist economic systems, such as Chayanov's, "might better explain the agrarian situation in much of the Third World today," as he put it (Sivakumar 2001: 54). Although taken up by some neo-marxists to help resolve contradictions in their own arguments, Chayanov's explanation was lost in its day amid a flood of opposition from Marxists (Lehmann, 1986). Its strength is its simplicity, and it has been used in a lot of modern literature, some of which goes far beyond the range Chayanov was arguing for, as Box 1.1 demonstrates. The real issue is with the kind of farm and the farming environment that Chayanov is arguing for.

Following Friedmann's (1980) analysis, further investigation into the strengths of the family farm model can be conducted. In the same way that capitalist farms benefit from price increases, fully commercial household farms are able to invest in labor-saving machinery and other innovations that can increase production. On the other hand, income declines are absorbed in various ways.

The family ranch can't promptly lessen its workforce, albeit individual individuals

may briefly pass on it to work for wages, or take occupations that can be reached from

home. They can cut back on investments in structures, tools, and machinery, but doing so will cost money in the long run if expansion is planned. In Chayanov's argument, they can and do reduce personal consumption or increase work inputs, exploiting themselves. They can also do both of these things if they want to buy new equipment or accumulate funds to expand their operations. They have a significant competitive advantage over farms that must make a profit and have a wage bill to pay because of this flexibility. According to Friedmann, the international competition in the wheat market that took place between the 1870s and the 1930s was a battle between capitalist and family farms, regardless of where they were located, in which the family farms won.

The findings of Friedmann and Mann and Dickinson (1978), who saw problems for capital on the land in the seasonal disjuncture of 6, should have led to a reframing of the agrarian question. Asking agrarian questions input from output. In the most capitalist of contexts, there have been additional in-depth analyses of how family farming manages its own "reproduction," such as Roberts's (1996) analysis of the southern high plains of the United States. However, Marx, Lenin, and

Kautsky are difficult to put to rest. Asking agrarian questions 7 BOX 1.1 SOME UNINTENDED CONSEQUENCES OF THEORIZING Kautsky, Lenin, and Chayanov were not writing for modern social scientists, so the original form of the question was reiterated.

However, in the 1960s and 1970s, all of their writings became crucial to agricultural debate in both developed and developing nations. The application of Chayanov's theory to farmers in developing nations has been particularly remarkable. The net (1993:

297) said that "Chayanov's model of a primarily self-sufficient

subsistence farm without wage labor and a household dedicated to its own reproduction" was appealing to anthropologists. Although it is true that Chayanov abstracted such a "natural" farm for theoretical discussion, he wrote in his main text that "the subject of our analysis is precisely [...]" a farm that has been drawn into the supply and demand of commodities "The peasant farm is acquisitive – an undertaking aiming at maximum income," as stated elsewhere (p. 119). The majority of his argument and data concern such farms.

Marshall Sahlins' (1972) "domestic mode of production" was based on Chayanov's discovery that the intensity of inputs on an independent family farm varies with the consumer/worker ratio. According to Ellis (1988a), a "domestic mode of production" is a dubious concept because a mode of production is something that emerges from the "social conditions of production" as a whole, not from the collection of distinct individual cases. Although he could have read more closely, Netting (1993) used Chayanov with greater care than Sahlins. In the Russian case, where Chayanov was primarily writing about land availability, he mentioned "land abundance" and noted significant differences between regions. Netting (1993) proceeded to peruse other Chayanovian attributes as

being 'independence, little ware creation or market investment,

what's more, no recruited work' (Mesh 1993: 311). Both Sahlins and Netting reproduced a straightforward Chayanov table to strengthen their arguments (1966: 78, tables 2 through 8), which we also reprint as Table 1.1. However, there is no such thing as a primitive self-sufficient economy represented by the data in this table. They are based on data from 1910 for a district that had the highest average net productivity (measured in terms of money) per annual worker in "labour agricultural economic units" of any of the 16 Russian districts (Chayanov 1966:

85, table 2–14). In Chapter 2, we will return to this district.

in some detail by Bernstein (2004), expressing hostility toward Griffin et al.'s new proposals for redistributive land reform (2002). In the meantime, the growing new dimension of agribusiness has been viewed as the farm's squeeze.

By providing inputs for farming, manufacturing, and handling outputs, capitalists have discovered investment opportunities that are more appealing than agricultural production itself. As a result, they have put money into agribusiness. Family farms—as well as small capitalist farms—continue to thrive as producers who are willing to take risks in exchange for trading with secure businesses in more controllable industries. Progressively,

agribusiness controls ranchers' exercises (Goodman and Redclift 1985; (Watts and Goodman, 1994)

Chayanov, similar to Lenin, perceived the effect of what was then called 'vendor

capital' and 'usury', both by vendors and more well off ranchers, on limited scope

Russian family ranchers. He proposed vertical integration of cooperative marketing to shield farmers from these harmful effects and provide them with scale trading benefits at the same time. Processing and marketing cooperatives have proven to be an effective means of overcoming the weakness of the unsupported individual farmer in some European countries (Lamartine-

Yates, 1940). In this, he drew on his extensive experience with cooperative marketing during the difficult conditions of World War I. They haven't been successful everywhere because they need a unique transactional regime that can't be easily created in places where it doesn't happen by itself. The preferred strategy in Russia was the horizontal integration of state and collective farming. However, under more recent neoliberal regimes, cooperation seems too much like discredited socialism to be popular. Although Chayanov's analysis was dynamic, it did not take classes into account. Lenin estimated that 20% of farmers operated in a capitalist manner, but he only wrote about the "middle peasants" and treated the entire farming population as one. Stalin disagreed with his preference for voluntary cooperatives as a path forward. As a result, there were allegations that he was attempting to undermine national farm production. Along with several of his colleagues, including the distinguished Kondratieff of "long cycle," he was arrested at the end of 1930 and died in the Gulag in 1939.

When discussing the competition for labor between agriculture as a whole and other economic sectors, Collantes (2006a) drew inspiration from a different source. Wolf (1982) shows how capitalist enterprises drew labor out of agriculture because the modern nonagricultural sector offered the prospect of higher living standards, simpler work routines, and the availability of leisure activities rather than just higher incomes when discussing the penetration of capitalism in developing nations.

Given this perception, a society based on family farming might be able to compete with capitalism in terms of commodity prices, capital markets, and land markets, but it might fail because it doesn't keep workers. When we come to de-agrarianization in Chapter 12, and then in our final arguments, we see the effect of this force for change. The most important agrarian issue today is, quite simply, how and under what circumstances has the family farm survived. The

subsequent stage is to examine what could appear glaringly evident and straightforward, however isn't - to characterize

the family ranch. The family ranch

The difficult 'center laborer' class of Lenin (1899) and Kautsky (1899), not one or the other entrepreneur nor ordinary, comprised of family ranchers. Between the large, industrially organized "capitalist farm" and the smaller allotments of paid workers employed in agriculture or elsewhere, the family farm stands. Many small-scale farmers, whether they own or rent land, maintain personal control over the land they farm. This is true for those who are referred to as "family farmers" in developed nations as well as those who are still frequently referred to as "peasants" in developing nations. The primary difference between the two is that commodities grown for sale and those grown for subsistence typically play at least equal roles. 727).

Frank Ellis provides a useful definition of "peasant farms" (1988a: 12) as "farm families, with access to their means of livelihood in land, utilizing primarily family labor in farm production, always located in a larger economic system, but fundamentally characterized by partial engagement in markets that tend to function with a high degree of imperfection." Family farms in developing nations are only truly distinguished from those in developed nations by the final of these criteria. Family farms also include what were once called "part-time farms," but are now more commonly referred to as "pluriactive" farms. On these farms, farmers and their families primarily rely on income from non-agricultural or off-farm sources. All of these to us are family farms.

Family farms are not all the same. They might be in the business of making money or they might only be a small part of the market. Commercial family farms differ primarily in that they are fully involved in the market and frequently employ family members in addition to wage workers or contractors. In order to comprehend the family farm's future viability, we will need to take into account the continuum that exists between each group. We pay little attention to corporate farms, despite the fact that these include truly family-owned farms that have been incorporated primarily for the purpose of simplifying taxation in the United States, the United Kingdom, the Netherlands, and a few other developed nations. Other farms have fictitious family ownership, with family members merely serving as prominent shareholders.6 These farms employ labor and are rarely run by family members; The majority use a manager. However, there is always a substantial "shadow-zone" and no distinct distinction is made. We recall the instance mentioned by Brookfield and Blaikie (1987: 229–30) of the US Deputy Secretary of Agriculture in 1986, whose official position would prevent him from receiving approximately $1,000,000 in California and Arizona state subsidies for his "family farm." Although he does represent an upper limit on the scale, the term "family farm" was undoubtedly a misnomer in his situation.

Family and industrialist ranches

To bind the meaning of a family homestead to endeavors that don't recruit outside

work would establish that such homesteads should be little in relative terms. This is overly simplistic due to the fact that many small farms employ one to a few laborers without transforming into anything like capitalist businesses. Due to family members' advancing age or illness, as well as their absence at work, it may become necessary to hire labor. Spending money in this way may be preferable to working long hours on the farm or even working at all. In Section 2 we depict how a few Chinese male 'ranchers' in 1938-39 had the option to invest their entire energy

in relaxation pursuits by exploiting work accessible at low wages and furthermore

of the neglected work of their spouses and little girls. However, they were not capitalists at all.

Hill (1993) made useful progress in determining what constitutes an operational "family farm," first noting that over 98% of all west-European farms are owned by individuals. He made use of a 1989 database from the European Union that listed annual farm labor. Non-family farms, also known as capitalist farms, were those on which hired workers who were not members of the farm's operating family provided more than half of the annual work input.

"Pure" family farms are only those where family members provided 95% or more of the annual work input. The remaining students belong to an intermediate class and contribute between 50% and 94% of their annual income through family work. In the twelve countries that were members of the European Union in 1989, family farms and intermediate farms made up 93.3% of all farms. According to Hill's definition, "non-family" farms only made up more than 15% of all farms in Britain and Spain.

There are issues with using official data because different countries use different thresholds to record farm data. Generally, farms of a very small size are not included, but Hill points out that almost all of those who are excluded belong to the family or the intermediate class. As in Australia, statistical thresholds may be altered. The "estimated value of farm operations" that serves as the foundation for the data was AUD 2,500 up until the middle of the 1980s. By 1996, it had increased twice to AUD 22,500. According to Garnaut and LimApplegate (1998), this resulted in a significant decrease in the number of farms that were recorded. However, as of 1996, an owner-manager ran 99 percent of the remaining arable, livestock, and dairy farms, with few making significant use of hired labor.

We consider family farms to be those that are owned or leased, are managed by a family, and have at least half of the annual work input performed by household members or other unpaid helpers (mostly neighboring farm household members working on a reciprocal basis), applying common sense to Hill's valuable efforts. During peak times and for specific skilled tasks, many family farms rely on paid labor or contract specialists. Some use gang labor, which is discussed in Chapter 4, or casual labor. We believe we are writing about the vast majority of all farms in the world, despite their diversity in most other respects, given the wide distribution of such family farms outside of state farming, surviving collective farms, and industrial plantations.

Besides, a verifiable view would recommend a propensity for family ranch activity to increment instead of decline; The regular use of unskilled farm labor has decreased significantly and continues to do so. In developed nations, wage labor is prohibitively expensive. While large capitalist businesses are compelled to cover these expenses, smaller businesses are increasingly unable to afford it.

10 Posing agrarian inquiries

The board of family ranches

While numerous ranchers own their territory, to some extent on contract or its same, they

seldom have full privileges to decide the way things are to be utilized. Their choices are further restricted by their agribusiness partners, as well as by national or more local laws.

Unless the law safeguards their rights, particularly their rights to improvements, tenants have less flexibility than owners to make changes. The rules governing land access vary greatly, and frequently, the actual practice diverges from the rules. As tenure and access conditions evolve over time, "customary rights" may ultimately become individual and inheritable tenure. Chapter 3 discusses everything.

The board of the singular ranch is frequently just notionally in the possession of the

senior male, in what is many times portrayed as a man centric example. In regions where men hold other jobs, farming households run by women are very common.

Following Netting, the farm is better regarded as a family business because the farmer's immediate family is typically involved in decision-making.

In this sense, a household is a group of people who live in the same building or group of buildings and share the cost or value of the farm's products. Occasionally, multiple nuclear families are involved. In the 1980s, 86% of the people living in a Bambara village in Mali lived in complex households with more than one married couple—sometimes even several— (Toulmin, 1992). In this excellent case the biggest families numbered up to

60 individuals. Also, keep in mind that Chayanov's family homes were larger than farms in Russia or other European countries today.

Although the members of a household may typically be kinship or affinity related, this is not always the case. Cases involving associated groups of related or unrelated individuals with patron-client relationships that can last a long time pose a more difficult question because they continue to depend on families who live and work on the same farm but typically in different buildings. Prior to the twentieth century, Japanese joint-family farms typically consisted of a landholding core surrounded by branch farms of affinal and cognatic relatives and various types of unrelated bond servants (T.C. Smith 1959).

Chayanov emphasizes the significance of household dynamism.

Natural families go through a cycle: they start out strong, grow as kids are born, and fall apart as kids get older and leave the family. However, individuals may leave the household for months or years to work and live elsewhere without officially dissolving the group. There is frequently a

cozy connection between the family cycle and the pattern of a ranch endeavor

from establishment through development to a static or perhaps declining stage. According to Roberts (1996), there are times when the farm as a whole is not transferred or inherited, as is the case on the southern high plains of the United States. As a result, the subsequent generation is required to reestablish its own farm businesses, thereby renewing the cycles of both the family and the business. This renewal does not occur suddenly upon the death or retirement of the previous holder; rather, it occurs over a period of approximately half a generation.

Agrarian inquiries No. 11: What size farm does a family own?

We arrive at a crucial issue here. A farm cannot be larger than the family can manage if it is to be operated for all regular purposes and primarily by family labor.

Between 1870 and 1935, family wheat farms in the American plains were able to grow significantly and actually thanks to machinery, which has continued to do so ever since the middle of the 20th century. But there are always limits at any technical level. Farm enterprise and farm size are related. As long as any short-term labor-intensive activities can be contracted out, livestock farming can be managed over larger areas with fewer workers than agricultural production. If the farm is too big, inefficiencies will always appear.

In addition, it is essential that the farm be large enough and that its businesses be requiring enough work for the willing and available family labor. The conditions are very different from place to place and over time. When the household is the primary body for organizing work and income rather than for consumption alone, Netting (1993) demonstrated that there is a very regular correspondence between household size and land size. He shows this a long ways past his self-restricted casing of

reference to smallholders.

Typically, the lower bound of the family range is violated, and poverty is frequently linked to this violation. Holdings with a lot less than one hectare rarely provide enough food for even a small family in rural areas around the world. However, their owners may view them as farms. In some Asian rice-growing regions, a family farm that is truly viable requires at least one hectare, but many farms do not reach this size.

On the other hand, there are family farms in Brazil's Amazon delta that are considered to be small despite occupying 30-40 ha of fields, forest, and land that has been left uncultivated. The ideal size for a farm shifts over time. According to Lamartine-Yates 1960, 70 percent of farms in a group of 15 European countries were less than 10 ha, despite the widespread belief in Europe as late as the 1950s that this was the minimum size necessary for a family farm operation to be viable. In the second half of the twentieth century, Lamartine-Yates argued that policy should aim for an average of 15 ha. However, by 1989, a family farm in Germany had a "utilized agricultural area" of 26 ha, according to Hill's strict definition. This was slightly larger than the average for west-Europe, but it was significantly smaller than the average for such farms in Britain, which was 66 ha (Hill, 1993). Box 1.2 provides additional context for the range's discussion.

Toward a dynamic and adaptable definition In terms of scale, the term "family farmer" must necessarily be relative to the typically capitalist "large farmers" in the region we are examining. We would distinguish the campesinos from the hacendados or latifundistas in the majority of Latin America. On the other hand, in a lot of sub-Saharan Africa, even the chiefs of many communities might be family farmers. There is a wide range in the size of family farms. The forms of 12 Asking agrarian questions about tenure are also extremely diverse, and farms frequently contain land that is tenured in various ways. Ranch development frequently appears as leasing in, and

withdrawal of leasing. The dynamism of land tenure arrangements, as well as all other aspects of the farm, is demonstrated by the examples cited here and in chapters 2 and 3. In the more business economies, dynamism reaches out to moves

both into and out of the industrialist and family methods of creation. The questionable data can be used by academics and journalists to draw conclusions (for instance, The Asking agrarian questions 13 Box 1.2 FARM SIZE IN OTHER LANDS). In southeastern Australia, a family farm should be between 50 and 100 ha, depending on where it is located. The maximum size is around a few thousand hectares. Two brothers own a farm in central southern Queensland. They operate it as a single farm with large-scale machinery, covering 8,000 ha. In many countries, including Australia, where self-provisioning is not particularly important, the size of a farmer's farm income rather than the size of their land is what others consider to be a "small" farmer. According to Ellis (1988a), it is not appropriate to consider farm area to be equivalent to the economic size of farms as units of production because measuring farm area would necessitate information on the total volume of resources utilized in production. He, like nearly everyone else, decides that farm area is the only useful comparative measure.

Farm size changes can happen quickly and are sometimes hard to understand.

In the Chimbu region of highland Papua New Guinea, where a single small subclan lives, Brown et al. (According to the findings of a 1990 study, the average cultivated and uncultivated area of 28 household farms was 0.62 ha in 1958, 1.37 ha in 1965, and 1.42 ha in 1984. Even though family herds of pigs were raised using cultivated food, all work was done using hand tools at all times, there was no working livestock, and there was no machinery. The number of households had increased, with some going out of business and others emerging. Coffee cultivation, followed by the marketing of other produce, had led to significant commercialization. Inequalities decreased rather than increased despite a significant increase in average farm size.

The terms of tenure changed significantly elsewhere. Winarto (2004) found that all of the land in a rice-growing region on the northern coastal plain of Java was owned by a small group of people before 1960, but that a lot of people moved in after controlled irrigation was implemented, which brought about big changes. By 1992, only 32% of farming households owned their own land; the remainder acquired it through cash rentals, sharecropping, or other means. There had been a lot of fragmentation, and while 30% of cultivators only used a single plot, 49% of cultivators used two or three plots.

Many of the landless majority were still able to access the produce of the cultivated land thanks to a complex web of employment opportunities.

4 December 2004, The Economist: 34), which states that "farms are generally on the way out, squeezed by high land costs and low profits," but there are still new players entering the market.

The fact that the majority of farms are smaller units in comparison to the standards of the country, region, and time are the most important factors in defining the family farm. First, the farms must be managed by the family, even if they occasionally employ a significant number of employees. Although Gray (1998) discusses the "consubstantiation" of family with farm as giving the concept a deeper social meaning in such instances, we think that the fact that the farm has been passed down through generations is significantly less diagnostically significant. Except during peak times, the family that owns or manages the business should provide at least half of the labor input. The farm may produce all, some, or none of its own food for its own consumption. It could market all, some, or none of its products. Even if we had the data to apply them, actual statistical boundaries would obscure the more fundamental characteristics of the family farm, which is the most important principle of family organization. Notes 1: Marx's much later publication of Pre-capitalist Economic Formations (Marx, 1965), which was written while Capital I was being prepared, makes it clear that Marx also considered several different routes from both collective and independent forms of property organization to the separation of a class of capitalists from a class of proletarians.

2 Marxian financial aspects, similar to traditional and neo-old style financial matters, depends on great

contest as its functioning speculation. It also has a positive outlook because it believes that history is a record of material progress. Marxian economics was categorized as a variant of neo-classical economics by Seers (1979), who looked at other parallels and found that both were initially derived from Adam Smith and David Ricardo.

3 We try to stay away from the obscure terms derived from Marx and Lenin that Friedmann and others used in the "new sociology of agriculture" that developed in the 1970s and 1980s, heavily influenced by Marxist literature. The classics of the time, including Friedmann's papers, are now rarely referred to by modern sociologists (Buttel, 2001). This wave, which paralleled closely similar waves in other fields of social science, has now passed.

4 He respected the high level and moderate separation portrayed by Lenin (1899)

as deceptive, however letting it out as an optional and minor component. In the Russia of 1923–25, for obvious reasons, he did not mention Lenin by name. Instead, he only mentioned writers "of a recent period" or "the late nineteenth century."

5 Any student of introductory modern economics is likely to be familiar with the types of diagrams Chayanov used to present this equilibrium under various production and requirement levels. Ellis, on the other hand, presented

a set of diagrams that were both more informative and elegant (1988a: 102–19).

6 According to the law, a family farm corporation is one in which at least half of the shareholders and voting stockholders are members of a related family in Missouri and a few other states in the United States. The farm needs to be actively managed by at least one stockholder. According to Constanța et al., farming must account for two thirds of the company's profits. 2003: 82).

7 Too late to be included in the text, we found a paper by Schmitt (1991) that, after pointing out that

scale economies on family farms have been overestimated, draws attention to the high transaction costs of hired labor, giving family labor a cost advantage that has grown and is likely to continue.

14 Asking agrarian questions 2 Farming as it was Aside from theory, a glimpse of farming practice in the first half of the 20th century can provide some insight into how family farming functioned prior to the changes discussed in the following chapters. These changes included large-scale mechanization and chemicalization, collectivized farming in communist countries,

and the era of "economic development" in developing nations. Conditions in Asia, Europe, and Africa can be seen in two, three, and one of the glimpses. None of them are depicted as "typical." The information spans roughly 40 years and is presented chronologically rather than geographically. In four of the five cases, working livestock were utilized, and careful planning of labor inputs was required. Hand labor was a common feature. Past those comments, we let the

models represent themselves.

Kossho, Ibaraki Prefecture, Japan, in 1903–10 In 1910, the eldest son of the leading family in the small village of Kossho, in the Kanto plain north of Tokyo, wrote a "from life" novel about an impoverished family in his village for a Tokyo newspaper's serial publication (Nagatsuka, 1989). All of Nagatsuka's family's land was rented, and they owed a lot of money, mostly to his father. According to T.C. Smith (1959), the central character, Kanji, was the adopted son-in-law of a family that had previously owned its house-site. As a result, it is likely that he was a member of a minor "branch family" that was formed from the bonded servants (na go) of the sole principal family in the small village at some point during the major agrarian change that occurred between the years 1600 and 1800. In Japan, it was common for families without male heirs to adopt a son-in-law, who would then inherit the family's assets as well as its debts. Rice was used to pay both his rent and his debt. More than half of the crop from his one small wet rice field and a few small dry crop fields was taken in by it. Rice and barley, which were frequently combined with rice and served as the main ingredient in dishes, were grown on these uplands. Sorghum, soy, sweet potatoes, and a variety of vegetables were also planted by the majority of the village's farmers. The good ranchers sold

these, yet for poor people they were a fundamental wellspring of food during the months prior to the

principal reap. The poor farmers only had hoes and mattocks for field preparation and their own backs for load carrying, but some farmers had horses that were used for transportation and larger fields. The wealthy used a lot of fertilizer, especially expensive dried fish meal, while the poor only had their own composted night soil made from forest leaves and grass. Since the mid-nineteenth-century reforms divided the common forest among private owners, even the latter had to be paid for. Farmers frequently assisted one another with tasks in the field and traded tools when necessary. In wet rice fields, horses appear to have been shared for the final puddling of the soil.

Farmers who had sufficient resources to provide their helpers with a feast after the work was completed were the only ones who could obtain the more substantial labor required for large tasks, particularly the planting of rice seedlings.

To cultivate their 2.5 ha of productive land, Nagatsuka's own family employed live-in laborers. Each man signed a long-term contract. Although the nature of the contract is not specified, it appears to be comparable to that of the ho ko nin of the previous two centuries, with the wage sometimes being paid directly to the worker and sometimes in advance to the head of the contracted servant's family (Smith, 1959). The worker was provided with food and clothing as part of the contractual arrangement, both of which were of a higher quality than what the independent tenants and their families could afford. The contrast in living conditions is made abundantly clear by Nagatsuka's narrative. Before getting married, Kanji had joined that workforce as a young man, and he continued to do so until his contract was fulfilled. As adopted son-in-law, he received an inheritance after the mother of his wife passed away. After his wife's early death in 1903, Kanji's plan was to pay off their debts by contracting out the services of their teenage daughter, who ended up becoming Kanji's primary support. She became his housekeeper and foster mother for her young brother, as well as his equal partner in field work, within a year or two. Between the years 1903 and 1910, Kanji was able to support himself and his family by working on a casual basis to create new fields in the forest. This allowed them to survive and gradually improve their situation. Kanji was taking advantage of the fact that he was dependent on the family of his landlord in this way, giving him opportunities that not all of the poor in the village could get.

During the season, many smaller farmers worked paid jobs on larger farms, which caused them to fall behind on their own programs. Kossho lacked the widespread "put-out" industrial work that was common in many Japanese villages; however, the small town of Noda, 40 kilometers to the west, had a thriving soy sauce factory. Young people from Kossho frequently found work there, raising the village's agricultural wages. Now and again, there was

work accessible on stream dike support a few kilometers away, work

that paid so inadequately that the people who did it returned with practically no net improvement in

their monetary assets. Even though Tokyo was only 70 kilometers away, only the wealthy ever visited, and Kossho's farmers did not use the city as a place to work or live.

The village had one shop, but the villagers had to go to another, probably larger, community for services like a blacksmith or a doctor. There were a lot of rivalries and tensions, and gossip could be very hurtful. Kanji, who had not yet turned sixteen, was a particular target of this conversation because he had been helping himself to other farmers' crops.

As a result, major seasonal celebrations and ceremonies were the only occasions when the community gathered. However, despite the fact that the majority of its families were extremely poor, they were better off than those living on the other side of the river, on flood-prone alluvial land, and without nearby forest land. Now, all of this is gone. After World War II, Japan underwent a significant land reform, and motorized tillers and other small-farm equipment became widely available (Francks, 2005). Within the expanding metropolis, Kossho is now embraced.

Volokolamsk, Moscow Oblast, Russia, in the years 1910–13 In Chapter 1, we encountered Volokolamsk. Aleksandr Chayanov

(1925–1966) conducted significant research there in 1910–13, when it was completely rural. Today, it serves as the terminus of a commuter rail service to the outer suburbs from Moscow. Composing

about it during the 1920s, he portrayed conditions in that period like they were still

current 10 years after the fact. The conditions under which family farms of this type and during this time period made decisions regarding the allocation of land, work, and income are thoroughly examined in Chayanov's chapter 4, which focuses primarily on farm organization in Volokolamsk.

His book was published in 1925, and a fourth chapter was added. It was not included in the German-language 1923 edition. As a result, it predates the theoretical formulation discussed in Chapter 1.

Somewhat recently of the nineteenth 100 years, cultivating in Volokolamsk had gone through a few significant changes. The region between Moscow and the Baltic states had a long history of commercial flax cultivation for the dispersed linen industry. However, in the second half of the nineteenth century, it greatly expanded to meet the growing demand of the then-new factory-organized linen industry in Belfast, Ireland. By 1900, a world market centered in Belfast was largely supplied by Russian flax. It remained that way until 1914. Farmers in the Volokolamsk district, which had a rail connection to the Baltic port of Riga, seized these opportunities more vigorously than those in other flax-growing regions, making it one of the most prosperous districts. Farmers also started sowing grass with clover around 1890 to make workhorse and cattle feed more readily available and to add nitrogen to the soil before the difficult flax crop. According to Chayanov (1966), the cultivation of oats for feed decreased, and even the relative importance of rye for bread decreased.

Despite the fact that yield was variable and the cost just to some degree less in this way, flax became

the main harvest at Volokolamsk. It provided winter labor in pre-sale primary processing in order to extract the fiber by retting and scutching the plant to produce the small amount of commercially valuable material. The conventional regional crop rotation gradually gave way to individual farmer-created rotations that better suited the flax-based economy. In these rotations, flax always came before clover.

Middle peasants, like the ones who were described, did not primarily decide how they used their land. Unlike Lenin (1899), Chayanov was not concerned with differentiation. Field plots were Farming as it was 17 changed from time to time due to occasional re-partitions of commune land, and there was frequent renting, so land was not short in general. The family workforce was the primary factor in determining the scope of activity because there was little chance of hiring workers and a poorly developed system of collaborative labor exchange. The family's bundle of needs was determined by its dietary and other requirements, and a significant portion of it was purchased in this village. Crops for sale were determined by market conditions. In the context of a highly seasonal demand for labor, all other decisions were greatly interdependent on one another.

Work was finished with ponies or bulls. There were threshing machines, reapers, and sometimes reaper-binders available, as well as a variety of field implements, but no tractors yet. The first decision, given the labor that was available, was how much could be spread out throughout the farming year to avoid bottlenecks during peak seasons, particularly harvest time. In the event that the family established more than it would have been ready to reap,

indeed, even with nine-or ten-hour working days during the restricted collecting season, it

would squander its work except if it could recruit work. Crops with top work

prerequisite emerging simultaneously were a specific issue, to be kept away from as far as could really be expected. The entire undertaking would be much simpler to manage if the peak labor requirements could be separated. The mix of crops and the amount of land allotted to each crop were determined by these factors.

The crucial decision regarding the utilization of horses was a part of the same set of choices. One pony could work somewhere in the range of two and three hectares of land.

Throughout the year, there was a very uneven demand, and for several months, horses were only used for transport. When farmers only had a small amount of land, it was cheaper to hire a horse and a worker by the day than to pay for maintenance. Because most farms in central Russia only have a limited supply of natural feed and all livestock must be stall-fed for several months of the year, the cost of maintaining horses and cattle was a crucial factor.

Cattle were sometimes used as draft animals to supplement or even replace horses, but they were essential for providing manure to maintain the fertility of the arable land. The difficulties in providing feed affected every aspect of the farm.

The majority of the arable land consumed livestock manure in the form of fodder, while some of the farm provided fodder. There was not much meadow land in Moscow Oblast. This was the high value of the sown clover at Volokolamsk, where it supplied 37% of the livestock feed on representative farms. According to Chayanov (1966), oats, meadow hay, and straw provided the remainder. While even the littlest

ranches expected to keep one cow to create compost, homesteads could grow their domesticated animals creation with planted grass or roots, up as far as possible at which family and

employed work was accessible. A peculiar rotation that included a two-field share of pasture each year was developed by some farmers near the railroad.

Printed in Great Britain
by Amazon

17034453R00061